POSH PALACES and Horrible Hovels

Andrew Solway

First published in Great Britain by Raintree, Halley Court, Jordan Hill, Oxford OX2 8EJ, part of Harcourt Education.

Raintree is a registered trademark of Harcourt Education Ltd.

Editorial: Louise Galpine, Harriet Milles, and Rachel Howells
Design: Richard Parker and Tinstar Design www.tinstar.co.uk
Illustrations: Steve Weston
Picture Research: Ruth Blair
Production: Alison Parsons

Originated by Modern Age
Printed and bound in China by Leo Paper Group

ISBN 978 1 4062 0845 0 (hardback)
ISBN 978 1 4062 0853 5 (paperback)
12 11 10 09 08
10 9 8 7 6 5 4 3 2 1

British Library Cataloguing in Publication Data
Solway, Andrew
Tudor London : posh palaces and horrible hovels. - (Fusion history)
1. Dwellings - England - London - History - 16th century - Juvenile literature 2. London (England) - Social conditions - 16th century - Juvenile literature
942.1'05
A full catalogue record for this book is available from the British Library.

Acknowledgements
The publishers would like to thank the following for permission to reproduce photographs: Art Archive/ Cornelis de Vries p. **7**; Bridgeman pp. **4** (Woburn Abbey, Bedfordshire, UK), **8** (Private Collection/©Look and Learn), **11** (Musee des Beaux-Arts, Lille, France, Lauros/Giraudon), **16** (Victoria & Albert Museum, London, UK), **17** (Ashmolean Museum, University of Oxford, UK), **20-21** (Guildhall Library, City of London), **27** (Longleat House, Wiltshire, UK), **29** (Private Collection); Getty Images pp. **5** (Mansell Collection), **25** (Image Bank); Mary Evans Picture Library pp. **9**, **15**; Topfoto/Fotomas Index p. **13**; Wellcome Library, London p. **22**.

Cover photograph of Hampton Court Palace reproduced with permission of Getty Images/Robert Harding World Imagery. Photograph of sunbleached wooden door reproduced with permission of © 2007 JupiterImages Corporation.

Every effort has been made to contact copyright holders of any material reproduced in this book. Any omissions will be rectified in subsequent printings if notice is given to the publishers.

The publishers would like to thank Bill Mariott and Lynne Bold for their assistance with the preparation of this book.

Disclaimer
All the Internet addresses (URLs) given in this book were valid at the time of going to press. However, due to the dynamic nature of the Internet, some addresses may have changed, or sites may have changed or ceased to exist since publication. While the author and publishers regret any inconvenience this may cause readers, no responsibility for any such changes can be accepted by either the author or the publishers.

It is recommended that adults supervise children on the Internet.

Contents

Some words are printed in bold, **like this**. You can find out what they mean on page 30. You can also look in the box at the bottom of the page where they first appear.

An itchy start

You wake up. Ouch! You feel really itchy all over. Yuk, you have fleas! Your bed is hard and lumpy, and it *stinks*. Someone is banging on the door. They are telling you to get up. Where are you? What day is it?

Now you remember. It is April 3rd, 1599. You are staying in an **inn** in Tudor London. You are working for a rich **wool merchant**.

Queen Elizabeth I

In 1599 Queen Elizabeth I (right) was Queen of England. England was one of the richest and most important countries in the world. One reason for this was the wool trade. In Tudor times, all countries in Europe wanted to buy English wool. Wool merchants became rich.

docks places where ships tie up to unload

inn cross between a pub and a hotel, where people could drink and also sleep

wool merchant someone who buys and sells wool and woollen cloth

Yesterday you walked over 32 kilometres (20 miles) from your home in the country. You were leading a string of horses. They were carrying woollen cloth.

This print shows a wool merchant in his warehouse. He is counting his money.

When you arrived in London, you went to the **docks** on the River Thames. You unloaded the cloth. Then you went to an inn near London Bridge. You ate a spicy meat pie. Afterwards you stumbled off to bed. You fell asleep straightaway.

Visiting the docks

Breakfast is bread and butter and weak beer. Ugh! At home in the country you drink milk for breakfast. Afterwards, you walk to the **docks** on the River Thames. You must make sure the woollen cloth is safely loaded onto a ship.

The docks are an amazing sight. You have never seen so many ships! Horses are bringing cartloads of **goods** to the dockside. There are loud noises – and powerful smells! Men shout as they load goods on board the ships. There are smells of strange spices. But the strongest stench is the river. Pooh! It smells awful!

The woollen cloth is safely on board the ship. Now you have to take a message. The **wool merchant** needs to know that his cloth is safely loaded. He lives on London Bridge.

Tudor trade

Most of the wool from England was taken in ships from London docks to Antwerp, in Belgium. From there it was sold all over Europe. In Tudor times, London was the most important trading city in England. Tudor ships were also travelling further than ever before. They were discovering new lands. They were bringing back amazing new fruit, vegetables, and other goods.

goods things that are carried on carts, boats, and other transport

This painting shows the Golden Hind*, a famous Tudor ship. Most Tudor ships looked similar to the* Golden Hind.

London Bridge

London Bridge is the only bridge across the River Thames. It is a very unusual bridge. It is covered in buildings! Near the middle there is a **drawbridge**. It lifts up to let large boats through.

The buildings on London Bridge are very smart. Only rich people can afford to live in them. At ground level, there are shops. You can buy fine cloth, feathers for hats, and fancy shoes. But, oh pooh! The smell from the river is worse than ever.

In 1599 London Bridge is already nearly 400 years old. The bridge itself is stone, but the houses are mostly made of wood.

drawbridge section of a bridge that lifts up

The road over the bridge itself is *very* busy. There are carts and barrows. A herd of sheep is being driven across the bridge. Poor people are carrying baskets. Crowds of rich people are looking in the shops. A small boy slips through the crowds. You see him steal the purse of a well-dressed man.

Cutpurses and other thieves

In Tudor times people often carried their money in a purse tied to their belt. A "cutpurse" was a thief who stole purses by cutting them off people's belts. People hung their purses with bells to stop them. But a good cutpurse could even steal a purse with built-in "alarm bells". "Moll Cutpurse" (right) was a famous Tudor thief. She always wore men's clothes.

The wool merchant's house

You arrive at the **wool merchant**'s house. It is a tall building made with timber frames. A servant lets you in.

The merchant is a rich man. Colourful **tapestries** hang on the walls. The windows have glass panes. There are no glass windows in your farmhouse at home. Just wooden shutters that the wind whistles through!

More servants hurry past. They carry plates of roast meat on silver plates. You feel very hungry! You are taken to the wool merchant.

The merchant wears a robe trimmed with fur. He sits at a large table. Servants have put meat on silver plates in front of him. He drinks wine from a thick glass. You tell the merchant that his wool is safely loaded on to the ship.

Tudor food

The picture opposite shows a typical Tudor rich man's house. Servants are working hard in the kitchen. Rich people ate a lot of meat, poultry, and fish. Sometimes rich people even ate swans and peacocks! Vegetables were seen as food for poor people. The rich ate from silver plates, and used knives. Forks were not yet used in England.

Poor people did not often eat meat. They mainly ate cheese, butter, vegetables, and cheap bread. Sometimes the bread was made from ground-up acorns!

London streets

The **wool merchant** asks you to take a message to a **lawyer**. The lawyer works in Westminster. The merchant gives you money to take a boat there. You decide to keep the money and walk instead.

After 10 minutes, you almost wish you had taken the boat! The streets are filthy and narrow. They are packed with carts and animals. There are crowds of people. Most of them look quite poor. Their clothes are made of rough woollen cloth. Some of them do not wear shoes.

Sewers and rubbish

There were no sewers in Tudor London. A few richer houses had garderobes (a kind of toilet). There were a few public toilets. However, most people used chamber pots. They threw the poo out into the street. Pigs and red kites (a kind of bird) ate the rubbish.

lawyer someone who is trained in the law
sewer pipe or open channel carrying waste from bathrooms and toilets

The top parts of the houses stick out over both sides of the street. They almost meet in the middle. A horrible, smelly, brown liquid runs down the centre of the street. It is an open **sewer**. A woman leans out of an upstairs window. She throws out a bowlful of something nasty. It just misses you!

You notice a couple of boys following you. You are pretty sure they want to rob you. You clutch on to your money tightly!

Old St Paul's

At last, you come to a wider, better street. At the end you can see St Paul's Cathedral. It starts to rain. You take shelter inside the church.

The inside of St Paul's is more like a market than a church. There are stalls selling books and paper. There are merchants making business deals. There are men looking for work. There are even a couple of men on horses. They ride right through the church!

You walk through the cathedral. Outside is St Paul's Cross. Another crowd of people are listening to a priest. He is giving a **sermon**. The priest is talking about "knowing your place". What does this mean?

The priest says that God has created a "Great Chain". At the top of the chain is God. Next down are kings and queens. Then come bishops and priests, followed by **nobles**. At the bottom of the chain are labourers and poor people. The priest says that God will be angry with people who try to break out of their place in the chain. You don't feel very cheerful listening to him.
You decide to leave!

*St Paul's Cross was an open-air **pulpit** in the churchyard of the cathedral. Here a priest is giving a sermon.*

noble powerful person, such as a duke or knight
pulpit raised platform, usually in a church or chapel
rebel to fight against the queen or government
sermon talk on a religious subject

Knowing your place!

In Tudor times, only a few people were rich. Most people were desperately poor and led hard lives. But Tudor poor people did not often **rebel** against their hard lives. They believed they would be punished by God if they did.

The Fleet

Past St Paul's Cathedral you come to a bridge over the river Fleet. A man is being dragged over the bridge by two constables. Constables are men of the law. The man is well dressed. He looks quite wealthy. A woman and two small children follow behind.

Just before the bridge is a large, gloomy building. It is a prison! The man, woman, and children are pushed through an open door in the wall of the prison. The door slams shut behind them. What have they done wrong?

Fleet Prison was still a debtor's prison in 1808, when this picture was painted.

beheaded to have your head cut off
debts money owed to another person
executed killed for committing a crime

You ask a poor woman in the street. She tells you this is Fleet Prison. People who cannot pay their **debts** are locked up here. Sometimes their families are put in prison with them.

At some of the windows the prisoners stretch out their arms. They are begging for money. Prisoners have to pay for their keep in this prison. Prisoners who cannot pay are put in filthy cells below ground. They nearly always become sick and die.

Crime and punishment

Punishments for crimes were very harsh in Tudor times. People could be **executed** for stealing anything worth more than a shilling (a tiny amount of money). They could even be hanged for stealing birds' eggs! Common people were hanged. **Nobles** were **beheaded**. Big crowds went to watch. In this picture (right), the Earl of Strafford is being beheaded at Tower Hill.

The Royal Palace

You walk on quickly. You are glad to leave the stinking river and the prison behind. Now you have reached the Strand. This is the posh part of town! You can't see any poor people here.

There are fine palaces on both sides of the road. They belong to important **nobles**. At the end of the Strand is Whitehall Palace. This is where the queen lives. Dozens of **courtiers** are crossing the road. Courtiers are companions and advisors to the queen.

You have never seen such fabulous clothes! The men wear feathers in their hats. They wear tight, fancy jackets (**doublets**). Their **breeches** are puffed out like pumpkins.

The women wear **bodices**. Their wide skirts are made of expensive material. Both men and women wear **ruffs** around their necks. They are all talking in very posh voices. You can hardly understand them!

Posh clothes

In the 1590s, only rich people could afford to dress in fine clothes. A silk dress might cost over £80. Most people in Tudor England earned less than £10 in a whole year!

bodice stiff, sleeveless top worn by women over a blouse
breeches short, loose trousers
courtier companion and advisor to the king or queen
doublet kind of tight jacket
ruff folded, circular collar

The picture below shows the sorts of clothes that rich Tudors wore.

On the Thames

You reach Westminster Hall. This is the highest court of law in England. You find the **lawyer** you need. You give him the **wool merchant**'s message. He thanks you and gives you a **tip**.

Your job is done. You have the rest of the day to yourself. You decide to take a boat back to London Bridge. Down by the river, you find a boatman to take you.

You can't believe how crowded the River Thames is! There are large boats loaded with timber and animals. There are smaller boats carrying people. These people seem to be wealthy. Some of them even have musicians playing music to them!

Filthy river

In the 16th century, the River Thames was very dirty. A lot of London's waste was thrown or washed into it. The river stank! Rats lived by the dirty river. They carried terrible diseases. One of these diseases was the **plague**. But rich people still preferred to travel by river. They were frightened of the dirty, crowded, dangerous streets.

This is a view of the Thames and London Bridge. The river is busy with all kinds of boats.

Across the river

The boatman tells you about a new theatre across the river. It is called The Globe. You decide to go and watch a play. The boatman drops you off in Southwark.

This seems to be a very rough area of the city. The streets of Southwark are narrow and dirty. The houses are badly built and crammed together. Some look as if they might fall down. The filthy smell everywhere makes you feel sick.

This beggar has only one leg. Sadly, Tudor treatments could not help people like him.

You have never seen so many poor people in one place. Beggars pull at your arms as you go past. Some are so ragged they have almost no clothes left.

You peep inside an open doorway. The room has a dirt floor and no furniture. In the corner you see a small boy lying on a pile of dirty straw. He looks sick. An old woman sits beside him. She is spooning something into his mouth.

Some Tudor cures

The Tudors used some strange things to try to cure illnesses or complaints. Here are just a few:

Complaint	Tudor cure
Plague	Garlic, arsenic, lily root, and dried toad
Asthma (causing breathing problems)	The lungs of a fox washed in wine, herbs, and liquorice
Toothache	Rub hare's brains on to gums
Hair loss	Rub on burnt doves' poo, or the ashes of little frogs

The Globe

Soon you reach the Globe Theatre. It is a large, circular building. You pay a penny to go in. You stand downstairs in an open area. The stage has a roof held up by pillars. The richer people sit on the higher levels around the stage.

Now the play starts. It is called *A Midsummer Night's Dream*. It was written by a very popular playwright. His name is William Shakespeare. The play is great fun. There are all sorts of mix-ups. At one point a man turns into a donkey! But in the end everything is sorted out.

Tomorrow you will set off home again. Have you enjoyed your visit to Tudor London? Well – yes, in parts! You enjoyed the play. You enjoyed seeing all those rich people, and the boat ride. But you certainly won't miss the dirt, the crowds, and the horrible smells. You'll be glad to breathe some fresh country air!

The original Globe Theatre was burned down in 1613. In 1997 a new Globe Theatre (see picture, right) was opened in Southwark. You can stand and watch a play there just as people did in Tudor times.

bear-baiting when a group of dogs fought with a bear

joust when two knights on horseback charged at each other with long spiked poles

Having fun

There was plenty of entertainment in Tudor times. Both rich and poor went to the theatre. They also liked animal shows, especially **bear-baiting**. Rich people enjoyed **jousting** and hunting. Queen Elizabeth I's father, King Henry VIII, played tennis. This helped to make the game popular.

Tudor rich

In Tudor times, the rich liked to show off their wealth. They spent money on:

- huge feasts
- fine clothing
- artistic skills.

Huge feasts

At mealtimes the Tudor rich liked to have loads of food on their tables. This showed off how rich they were. There was usually far more food than anyone could eat. Rich nobles could spend about £3,500 a year on food. This was a huge sum of money for the time.

Fine clothing

In Tudor times there were special laws that said what people could wear. These were called "Sumptuary Laws". They said that only **noble** people could wear velvet, satin, or silver or gold lace. Even rich merchants were not allowed to wear these things. The government hoped these laws would keep people "in their place".

Artistic skills

The children of rich nobles trained to become **courtiers**. Courtiers are companions to a king or queen. Boys had to learn "to ride, **joust**, use all weapons, run, leap, dance, sing, and play all instruments tunefully …hunt and play tennis…" They were taught to speak French, Latin, Greek, Italian, and Spanish! The girls learned music, singing, dancing, and needlework.

This painting from 1567 shows Lord Cobham and his family at mealtime. You can tell they are a rich family. The children are eating fruit from silver plates. The parrot is a sign of Tudor travels to faraway lands.

Tudor poor

There were three groups of poor people in Tudor times:

- the helpless poor
- the able-bodied (healthy) poor
- "rogues and vagabonds".

The helpless poor

These were the old, the sick, and children. They were given a little money and some food each week. Children of the helpless poor were taught work skills. People believed it was not their fault that they were poor.

"Rogues and vagabonds"

These were people who could work but preferred to beg or steal. This group were the most likely to make trouble! It was against the law to beg outside your own **parish**. Anybody found begging away from home was whipped "until his back was bloody". People who kept on begging could be sent to prison or hanged.

The able-bodied poor

These were healthy people who wanted work but could not find any. Each parish had to build a workhouse. The able-bodied poor worked in these workhouses. They made useful things like cloth. They stayed in the workhouses until they found a proper job.

parish small area with its own church

This picture from the 1560s shows a beggar being whipped through the streets.

Helping the poor

In Tudor times, rich people were frightened of poor people – because there were so many of them! They thought poor people might **rebel**. In 1597 the government decided poor people should be helped. Rich people had to pay a tax (money to the government). It was called the Poor Rate. The money was given to the poor. This might stop them causing trouble for the rich.

Glossary

bear-baiting when a group of dogs fought with a bear. People bet on whether the dogs or the bear would win.

beheaded to have your head cut off. Noblemen and women were beheaded for serious crimes such as treason.

bodice stiff, sleeveless top worn by women over a blouse

breeches short, loose trousers. Fashionable men wore their breeches very short and gathered into the leg at the bottom.

courtier companion and advisor to the king or queen

debts money owed to another person

docks places where ships tie up to unload

doublet kind of tight jacket. Men wore a doublet over their shirt.

drawbridge section of a bridge that lifts up

executed killed for committing a crime

goods things that are carried on carts, boats, and other transport

hose long wool or silk stockings, reaching to the top of the legs

inn cross between a pub and a hotel where people could drink and also sleep

joust when two knights on horseback charged at each other with long spiked poles

lawyer someone who is trained in the law

noble powerful person, such as a duke or knight. Noblemen and women worked for the king or queen.

parish small area with its own church

plague disease that killed many people in Tudor times. It was often called the Black Death because it gave people black sores on their skin.

pulpit raised platform, usually in a church or chapel. Priests give their sermons from pulpits.

rebel to fight against the queen or government

ruff folded, circular collar

sermon talk on a religious subject. Sermons are usually based on the Bible.

sewer pipe or open channel carrying waste from bathrooms and toilets

tapestry picture that is sewn or woven into a piece of cloth

tip present of a small amount of money

wool merchant someone who buys and sells wool and woollen cloth

Want to know more?

Books to read

People in the Past: Tudor Rich and Poor, Haydn Middleton (Heinemann Library, 2004)

Real Lives: Tudor Children, Sally Purkis (A&C Black, 2004)

Shakespeare's Globe, Toby Forward (Walker Books, 2005)

Websites

http://elizabethan.org/compendium

This site has information about Elizabethan England in entertaining, bite-sized chunks.

http://mapoflondon.uvic.ca

The Map of Early Modern London was drawn in 1643. Click on sections to see close-ups, with information about the places shown.

www.oldlondonbridge.com/history.shtml

On this website, the London Bridge Museum presents an illustrated history of London Bridge, from Roman times to the present day.

Find out more about the smelly River Thames in ***The Great Stink***.

Read about one of history's most famous round-the-world voyages in ***Captain's Log***.

Index